WHAT I KNOW ABOUT

THE
AMERICAN
DREAM

Gibbs Smith

First Edition
29 28 27 26 25   5 4 3 2 1

Compilation © 2025 Gibbs Smith

Published by
Gibbs Smith
570 N. Sportsplex Dr.
Kaysville, Utah 84037

1.800.835.4993 orders
www.gibbs-smith.com

Designed by Sheryl Dickert
Printed and bound in China

This product is made of FSC®-certified and other controlled material.

MIX
Paper | Supporting
responsible forestry
FSC   FSC® C208677
www.fsc.org

Library of Congress Control Number: 2024941806

ISBN: 978-1-4236-6842-8

INTRODUCTION

As America approaches its 250th anniversary, it is the perfect time to ponder the ideals upon which this country was founded: democracy, independence, and freedom.

What I Know About the American Dream brings together 125 quotes from America's Founding Fathers, First Ladies, presidents, and politicians, along with inspiring words of wisdom from abolitionists, inventors, artists, writers, and thinkers.

Susan B. Anthony, Frederick Douglass, George Washington, Eleanor Roosevelt, and Ralph Waldo Emerson, among many others, share insights, inspiration, and questions that remind us to look at our values as Americans and both the hopes and realities of the American Dream.

These quotes from some of America's greatest leaders and thinkers will teach and inspire us, as well as remind us of our responsibilities to our country and to each other.

We hold these truths to be self-evident:

that all men are created equal; that they

are endowed by their Creator with certain

unalienable rights; that among these are

life, liberty, and the pursuit of happiness.

—DECLARATION OF INDEPENDENCE

To me, the American Dream is being able to follow your own personal calling. To be able to do what you want to do is incredible freedom.

—MAYA LIN, ARCHITECT

Be courageous. I have seen many depressions

in business. Always America has emerged

from these stronger and more prosperous . . .

Have faith! Go forward!

—THOMAS EDISON, INVENTOR AND BUSINESSMAN

America is woven of many strands. I would recognize them and let it so remain. Our fate is to become one, and yet many. This is not prophecy, but description.

—RALPH ELLISON, AMERICAN WRITER

To realize the American Dream, the most important thing to understand is that it belongs to everybody. It's a human dream. If you understand this and work very hard, it is possible.

—CRISTINA SARALEGUI, JOURNALIST

Those who won our independence ... believed liberty to be the secret of happiness and courage to be the secret of liberty.

—LOUIS D. BRANDEIS, U.S. SUPREME COURT JUSTICE

True patriotism lies in the belief that

our country can always strive for better.

—BETSY ROSS, AMERICAN SEAMSTRESS

The American Dream is that dream of

a land in which life should be better

and richer and fuller for everyone.

—JAMES TRUSLOW ADAMS, AMERICAN WRITER AND HISTORIAN

There are those who will say that the liberation of humanity, the freedom of man and mind is nothing but a dream. They are right.

It is the American Dream.

—ARCHIBALD MACLEISH, AMERICAN POET AND WRITER

I'm the daughter of refugees.

The immigrant mentality is to work hard,

be brave, and never give up in your pursuit

of achieving the American Dream.

—RESHMA SAUJANI, ACTIVIST

IS ANOTHER NAME FOR OPPORTUNITY.

—RALPH WALDO EMERSON, AMERICAN ESSAYIST

I won't be happy until we have every boy in

America between the ages of six and sixteen

wearing a glove and swinging a bat.

—BABE RUTH, AMERICAN BASEBALL PITCHER

America, to me, is freedom.

—WILLIE NELSON, AMERICAN COUNTRY SINGER

I hold it, that a little rebellion, now and then,

is a good thing, and as necessary in the

political world as storms in the physical.

—THOMAS JEFFERSON, AMERICAN PRESIDENT

You can't fight for your rights if you don't know what they are.

—JOHN ROBERTS, U.S. SUPREME COURT JUSTICE

True patriotism springs from a belief in the dignity of the individual—freedom and equality not only for Americans but for all people on earth.

—ELEANOR ROOSEVELT, FIRST LADY

The way to be patriotic in America is not only
to love America, but to love the duty that
lies nearest to our hand, and to know that in
performing it we are serving our country.

—WOODROW WILSON, AMERICAN PRESIDENT

We cannot build our own

future without helping

others to build theirs.

—BILL CLINTON, AMERICAN PRESIDENT

WHEN THE YOUTH OF AMERICA GETS TOGETHER, AMAZING THINGS HAPPEN.

—TOM FORD, FASHION DESIGNER AND FILMMAKER

We have become not a melting pot but a beautiful mosaic.

Different people, different beliefs, different yearnings,

different hopes, different dreams.

—JIMMY CARTER, AMERICAN PRESIDENT

We are bound together by the most powerful of all ties, our fervent love for freedom and independence, which knows no homeland but the human heart.

—GERALD FORD, AMERICAN PRESIDENT

We are given power not to advance our own purposes nor to make a great show in the world, nor a name. There is but one just use of power and it is to serve people.

—GEORGE W. BUSH, AMERICAN PRESIDENT

"

Patriotism is easy to understand in

America. It means looking out for yourself

by looking out for your country.

—CALVIN COOLIDGE, AMERICAN PRESIDENT

"

The American Dream can

no more remain static than

can the American nation.

—ELEANOR ROOSEVELT, FIRST LADY

The life of the nation is secure only while the nation is honest, truthful, and virtuous.

—FREDERICK DOUGLASS, AMERICAN ABOLITIONIST AND STATESMAN

I think America signifies opportunity.

—AUDRA MCDONALD, AMERICAN SINGER AND ACTRESS

America's present need is

not heroics but **healing**;

not nostrums but **normalcy**;

not revolution but **restoration**.

—WARREN G. HARDING, AMERICAN PRESIDENT

It's never paid to bet against America.

We come through things, but it's not

always a smooth ride.

—WARREN BUFFETT, AMERICAN BUSINESSMAN

The greatness of America lies not in being more enlightened than any other nation, but rather in her ability to repair her faults.

—ALEXIS DE TOCQUEVILLE, WRITER AND POLITICAL PHILOSOPHER

In America nobody says you have to keep

the circumstances somebody else gives you.

—AMY TAN, AMERICAN AUTHOR

AMERICA WAS NOT BUILT ON FEAR.

America was built on courage,

on imagination, and an unbeatable

determination to do the job at hand.

—HARRY S. TRUMAN, AMERICAN PRESIDENT

I travel the world, and I'm happy to

say that America is still the great

melting pot—maybe a chunky stew

rather than a melting pot at this

point, but you know what I mean.

—PHILIP GLASS, AMERICAN COMPOSER

What the people want is very simple—

they want an America as good as its promise.

—BARBARA JORDAN, U.S. REPRESENTATIVE

America is more than a place.

More significant, it is an idea.

—PAUL GREENBERG, AMERICAN AUTHOR

Liberty means responsibility.

That is why most men dread it.

—GEORGE BERNARD SHAW, PLAYWRIGHT AND CRITIC

YOU CANNOT BUILD CHARACTER AND COURAGE BY TAKING AWAY A MAN'S INITIATIVE AND INDEPENDENCE.

—ABRAHAM LINCOLN, AMERICAN PRESIDENT

If freedom of speech is to be taken away

then dumb and silent we may be led,

like sheep to the slaughter.

—GEORGE WASHINGTON, FIRST PRESIDENT OF THE UNITED STATES

If an immigrant comes here in good faith, he becomes an American and assimilates himself to us. He will be treated on an exact equality with everyone else, for it is an outrage in America to discriminate against any such man because of creed, birthplace, or origin.

—THEODORE ROOSEVELT, AMERICAN PRESIDENT

The cost of freedom is always high, but Americans have always paid it.

—JOHN F. KENNEDY, AMERICAN PRESIDENT

And so, my fellow Americans:

ask not what your country can do for you—

ask what you can do for your country.

—JOHN F. KENNEDY, AMERICAN PRESIDENT

Injustice anywhere is a threat

to justice everywhere.

—MARTIN LUTHER KING, JR., CIVIL RIGHTS LEADER

Better to fight for SOMETHING than live for NOTHING.

—GEORGE PATTON, U.S. ARMY GENERAL

As the happiness of the people is the sole end of government, so the consent of the people is the only foundation of it, in reason, morality, and the natural fitness of things.

—JOHN ADAMS, AMERICAN PRESIDENT

No man is good enough to govern another man, without that other's consent.

—ABRAHAM LINCOLN, AMERICAN PRESIDENT

I prayed for freedom for twenty years, but received

no answer until I prayed with my legs.

—FREDERICK DOUGLASS, AMERICAN ABOLITIONIST AND STATESMAN

A patriot must always be ready to defend his country against his government.

—EDWARD ABBEY, WRITER AND ENVIRONMENTALIST

What is the essence of America?

Finding and maintaining that perfect, delicate balance

between freedom "to" and freedom "from."

—MARILYN VOS SAVANT, AMERICAN COLUMNIST

Fight for the things that you care about,

but do it in a way that will lead others to join you.

—RUTH BADER GINSBURG, U.S. SUPREME COURT JUSTICE

AMERICA IS A TUNE.

It must be sung together.

—GERALD STANLEY LEE, AMERICAN WRITER AND MINISTER

Part of America's genius has always been its ability

to absorb newcomers, to forge a national identity

out of the disparate lot that arrived on our shores.

—BARACK OBAMA, AMERICAN PRESIDENT

In America, anyone can become president.

That's the problem.

—GEORGE CARLIN, COMEDIAN AND SOCIAL CRITIC

In America you can say anything you want— as long as it doesn't have any effect.

—PAUL GOODMAN, AMERICAN WRITER

America did not invent human rights. In a very real sense, it is the other way round. Human rights invented America.

—JIMMY CARTER, AMERICAN PRESIDENT

It is the immigrant hordes who keep this country

alive, the waves of them arriving year after year . . .

Who believes in America more than the people who

run down the gangplank and kiss the ground?

—E. L. DOCTOROW, AMERICAN NOVELIST

I think, with never-ending gratitude, that the young women of today do not and can never know at what price their right to free speech and to speak at all in public has been earned.

—LUCY STONE, WOMEN'S RIGHTS ACTIVIST

MY COUNTRY IS THE WORLD,

———————— AND ————————

MY RELIGION IS TO DO GOOD.

—THOMAS PAINE, FOUNDING FATHER

The bosom of America is open to receive not only the opulent and respectable Stranger, but the oppressed and persecuted of all Nations and Religions; whom we shall welcome to a participation of all our rights and privileges.

—GEORGE WASHINGTON, FIRST PRESIDENT OF THE UNITED STATES

While I take inspiration from the past, like most Americans, I live for the future.

—RONALD REAGAN, AMERICAN PRESIDENT

Nowhere on the globe do men live so well as in America, or grumble so much.

—HENRY WARD BEECHER, AMERICAN CLERGYMAN

[AMERICA IS]

the land where people find

whatever they have lost.

—GÜNTER GRASS, NOVELIST

This is America . . .

a brilliant diversity spread like stars,

like a thousand points of light in a

broad and peaceful sky.

—GEORGE H. W. BUSH, AMERICAN PRESIDENT

//

It was we, the people; not we, the white male citizens; nor yet we, the male citizens; but we, the whole people, who formed the Union. And we formed it, not to give the blessings of liberty, but to secure them; not to the half of ourselves and the half of our posterity, but to the whole people—women as well as men.

—SUSAN B. ANTHONY, WOMEN'S RIGHTS ACTIVIST

//

In this country, there is an opportunity for the development of man's intellectual, cultural, and spiritual potentialities . . . I mean not simply an opportunity for greatness for a few, but an opportunity for greatness for the many.

—EDWIN H. LAND, SCIENTIST AND INVENTOR

What joins the Americans one to another is not a common ancestry, language, or race, but a shared work of the imagination that looks forward to the making of a future, not backward to the insignia of the past.

—LEWIS H. LAPHAM, AMERICAN WRITER

Always praising America is not patriotism. It is idolatry.

But always criticizing America is not patriotism, either.

It is ingratitude. The former is blind to America's faults;

the latter is blind to America's virtues.

—MARK GERZON, WRITER AND POLITICAL MEDIATOR

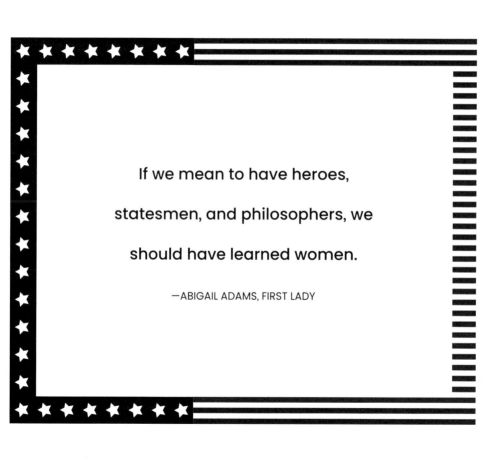

If we mean to have heroes,

statesmen, and philosophers, we

should have learned women.

—ABIGAIL ADAMS, FIRST LADY

Freedom makes a huge requirement of every human being. With freedom comes responsibility. For the person who is unwilling to grow up, the person who does not want to carry his own weight, this is a frightening prospect.

—ELEANOR ROOSEVELT, FIRST LADY

We should keep steadily before our minds the fact that Americanism is a question of principle, of purpose, of idealism, of character; that it is not a matter of birthplace, or creed, or line of descent.

—THEODORE ROOSEVELT, AMERICAN PRESIDENT

This nation, under God, shall have a new birth of freedom—and that government of the people, by the people, for the people, shall not perish from the earth.

—ABRAHAM LINCOLN, AMERICAN PRESIDENT

If liberty means anything at all,

it means the right to tell people

what they do not want to hear.

—GEORGE ORWELL, NOVELIST

We must be free not because we claim freedom, but because we practice it.

—WILLIAM FAULKNER, AMERICAN WRITER

For to be free is not merely to cast off one's chains, but to live in a way that respects and enhances the freedom of others.

—NELSON MANDELA, POLITICIAN AND ANTI-APARTHEID ACTIVIST

Those who would give up essential liberty to purchase a

little temporary safety deserve neither liberty nor safety.

—BENJAMIN FRANKLIN, FOUNDING FATHER

By ensuring that no one in government has too much power, the Constitution helps protect ordinary Americans every day against abuse of power by those in authority.

—JOHN ROBERTS, U.S. SUPREME COURT JUSTICE

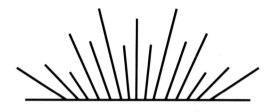

Give freely of yourself always to your family,

your friends, your community, and your country.

The world will pay you back many times over.

—SANDRA DAY O'CONNOR, U.S. SUPREME COURT JUSTICE

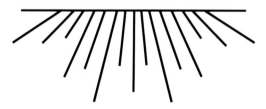

If you assume that there is an instinct

for freedom, there are opportunities to

change things, there's a chance you may

contribute to making a better world.

THE CHOICE IS YOURS.

—NOAM CHOMSKY, PROFESSOR AND POLITICAL ACTIVIST

But laws alone cannot secure freedom of expression; in order that every man may present his views without penalty there must be a spirit of tolerance in the entire population.

—ALBERT EINSTEIN, SCIENTIST

While we are contending for our own liberty, we should be very cautious not to violate the rights of conscience in others.

—GEORGE WASHINGTON, FIRST PRESIDENT OF THE UNITED STATES

Wars may be fought with weapons, but they are won by men. It is the spirit of men who follow and of the man who leads that gains the victory.

—GEORGE PATTON, U.S. ARMY GENERAL

Freedom is not worth having if it does not include the freedom to make mistakes.

—MAHATMA GANDHI, CIVIL RIGHTS WORLD LEADER

Disobedience is the true foundation of liberty.

The obedient must be slaves.

—HENRY DAVID THOREAU, WRITER AND NATURALIST

When injustice becomes law, resistance becomes duty.

—RUTH BADER GINSBURG, U.S. SUPREME COURT JUSTICE

Those who expect to reap the blessings

of freedom, must . . . undergo the

fatigues of supporting it.

—THOMAS PAINE, FOUNDING FATHER

SHOW ME THAT AGE AND COUNTRY WHERE THE RIGHTS AND LIBERTIES OF THE PEOPLE WERE PLACED ON THE SOLE CHANCE OF THEIR RULERS BEING GOOD MEN, WITHOUT A CONSEQUENT LOSS OF LIBERTY?

—PATRICK HENRY, *FOUNDING FATHER*

America is a leap of the imagination.

From its beginning, people had only a persistent idea of

what a good country should be. The idea involved freedom,

equality, justice, and the pursuit of happiness.

—IAN FRAZIER, AMERICAN WRITER

Patriotism is a commitment to what

is best inside us all.

—VERA NAZARIAN, WRITER

You've got to

VOTE, VOTE, VOTE, VOTE.

That's it; that's the way we move forward.

That's how we make progress for ourselves and for our country.

—MICHELLE OBAMA, FIRST LADY

FREEDOM

is a word like "love" or "health"

that teeters on the edge of cliché until

you don't have one or the other and

you wish like hell that you did.

—TERRY TEMPEST WILLIAMS, WRITER AND ENVIRONMENTALIST

If the Bill of Rights contains no guarantee

that a citizen shall be secure against

lethal poisons distributed either by private

individuals or by public officials, it is surely

only because our forefathers, despite their

considerable wisdom and foresight, could

conceive of no such problem.

—RACHEL CARSON, WRITER AND ENVIRONMENTALIST

America is great because she is good.

If America ceases to be good, America

will cease to be great.

—ALEXIS DE TOCQUEVILLE, WRITER AND POLITICAL PHILOSOPHER

Because of what America is and what America has done, a firmer courage, a higher hope, inspires the heart of all humanity.

—CALVIN COOLIDGE, AMERICAN PRESIDENT

AMERICA

is civilization,

progress, and

technology.

—KARIMA KAMAL, JOURNALIST

What America surely needs now is a return to those original ideals that have been the sources of her greatness.

—ARNOLD TOYNBEE, HISTORIAN

Freedom lies in being bold.

—ROBERT FROST, AMERICAN POET

I love America more than any other country in the world, and, exactly for this reason, I insist on the right to criticize her perpetually.

—JAMES BALDWIN, WRITER AND CIVIL RIGHTS ACTIVIST

The essence of America—that which really unites us—is not ethnicity, or nationality, or religion—it is an idea—and what an idea it is: That you can come from humble circumstances and do great things.

—CONDOLEEZZA RICE, U.S. SECRETARY OF STATE

Jazz music is America's past and its potential, summed up and sanctified and accessible to anybody who learns to listen to, feel, and understand it.

—WYNTON MARSALIS, JAZZ MUSICIAN

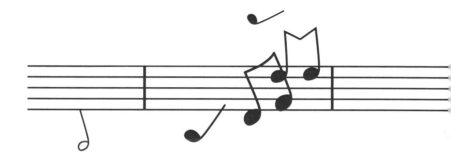

I don't know what America would be

without New Orleans and the music.

—TROMBONE SHORTY, MUSICIAN

We must not confuse dissent with disloyalty. When the loyal opposition dies, I think the soul of America dies with it.

—EDWARD R. MURROW, JOURNALIST AND WAR CORRESPONDENT

What's right about America is that although we have

a mess of problems, we have great capacity—intellect

and resources—to do something about them.

—HENRY FORD, AMERICAN INDUSTRIALIST

If we want to be proud to be from a country like America and all the things that we hang our hats on, like diversity, equality, land of the free and home of the brave, it's everybody's responsibility to ensure that everyone in the country is being afforded the same rights.

—MEGAN RAPINOE, AMERICAN SOCCER PLAYER

America's greatest strength has always been

its hopeful vision of human progress.

—JOHN MCCAIN, U.S. SENATOR

America is not just a power,

it is a promise. It is not enough for our

country to be extraordinary in might;

it must be exemplary in meaning.

—NELSON ROCKEFELLER, U.S. VICE PRESIDENT

Democracy is not just the right to vote,

it is the right to live in dignity.

—NAOMI KLEIN, AUTHOR AND SOCIAL ACTIVIST

There is no more vital right in a

democracy than the right to vote.

Without it, no other right is secure.

—LAWRENCE GOLDSTONE, WRITER

You cannot value dreams according to the odds of their coming true. The real value is in stirring within us the will to aspire.

—SONIA SOTOMAYOR, U.S. SUPREME COURT JUSTICE

[America] values

tolerance, cooperation,

learning, and the

amicable resolution

of conflicts.

—SAMUEL ALITO, U.S. SUPREME COURT JUSTICE

The nation behaves well if it treats the natural resources as assets which it must turn over to the next generation increased and not impaired in value.

—THEODORE ROOSEVELT, AMERICAN PRESIDENT

THIS IS YOUR DEMOCRACY.

Make it. Protect it. Pass it on.

—THURGOOD MARSHALL, U.S. SUPREME COURT JUSTICE

Where liberty is, there is my country.

—BENJAMIN FRANKLIN, FOUNDING FATHER

The fact is, with every friendship

you make, and every bond of trust

you establish, you are shaping

the image of America projected

to the rest of the world.

—MICHELLE OBAMA, FIRST LADY

FREEDOM IS NOTHING BUT A CHANCE TO BE BETTER.

—ALBERT CAMUS, WRITER

AMERICA IS HOPE.

IT IS COMPASSION.

IT IS EXCELLENCE.

IT IS VALOR.

—PAUL TSONGAS, U.S. SENATOR

Americans never quit.

We never surrender.

We never hide from history.

We make history.

—JOHN MCCAIN, U.S. SENATOR

There is one thing that the American people

always rise to and extend their hand to, and that is

the truth of justice and of liberty and of peace.

—WOODROW WILSON, AMERICAN PRESIDENT

Patriotism consists not in waving the flag,

but in striving that our country shall

be righteous as well as strong.

—JAMES BRYCE, POLITICIAN

The Constitution of the United States was made not merely

for the generation that then existed, but for posterity—

unlimited, undefined, endless, perpetual posterity.

—HENRY CLAY, U.S. SENATOR AND STATESMAN

I BELIEVE IN AMERICA BECAUSE WE HAVE GREAT DREAMS, AND BECAUSE WE HAVE THE OPPORTUNITY TO MAKE THOSE DREAMS COME TRUE.

—WENDELL WILLKIE, POLITICIAN

Dreams are the foundation of America.

—LUPITA NYONG'O, ACTRESS

In the truest sense,

freedom cannot be bestowed;

it must be achieved.

—FRANKLIN D. ROOSEVELT, AMERICAN PRESIDENT

The American Dream does not come to those who fall asleep.

—GERALD FORD, AMERICAN PRESIDENT

Heroism doesn't always happen in a burst of glory. Sometimes small triumphs and large hearts change the course of history.

—MARY ROACH, AMERICAN AUTHOR

A GOOD SONG REMINDS US

WHAT WE'RE FIGHTING FOR.

—PETE SEEGER, SINGER-SONGWRITER

I think of a hero as someone who understands the degree of responsibility that comes with his freedom.

—BOB DYLAN, SINGER-SONGWRITER

And so even though we face the difficulties of today and tomorrow, I STILL HAVE A DREAM. It is a dream deeply rooted in the American Dream.

—MARTIN LUTHER KING, JR., CIVIL RIGHTS LEADER